*Inspired by and dedicated to
the Heart and Soul of the Feminine*

Sleeping with Sophia

A Collection of Poems
For the Love of Earth & Woman

Henk Brandt

HENK BRANDT

Maidenhair Books

Maidenhair Books
Published by Haecceity Press, LLC
Charleston, SC 29401

The Maidenhair image is a registered trademark.
The trade name, Maidenhair Books, is a registered trademark.
Haecceity Press is a registered trademark.

All rights are reserved and protected. No part of this book may be used or reproduced in any manner whatsoever without written approval except in the case of brief quotations embodied in critical articles and reviews.

Acknowledgement and Permissions printed on last page

Library of Congress Cataloging-in-Publication Database

Brandt, Henk
   Sleeping with Sophia: A Collection of Poems / For the Love of Earth & Woman
   About Women and the Archetypal Feminine

FIRST EDITION

Book design by Cristina Young
Composed by Graphic Composition, Inc., Bogart, Georgia
Editing by Harriet McDougal, Mark Nepo, and Susan Hull Walker

ISBN 978-0-9839276-1-7
Copyright © 2013 by Henk Brandt
All Rights Reserved
Printed in The United States of America
Haecceity Press LLC, 2013

PREFACE

As expressed by the title of this book, these poems are about Sophia. But *who* is Sophia? Very likely she is the woman on the cover whose Mona Lisa smile arouses curiosity. Perhaps, the woman tends a secret, something deliciously mysterious, to be revealed within these pages.

The name Sophia interests me because it refers to the ancient goddess of Wisdom mentioned in the Book of Proverbs. "Sophia" in ancient Greek literally means Wisdom—the kind of Wisdom that is commonly referred to as Perennial Wisdom, Sacred Wisdom or the Wisdom of the Ages. Yet, many of us are finding that Wisdom itself is changing rapidly before our eyes to include the breathtaking emergence of a decidedly *feminine* form of consciousness that by its very nature dramatically expands the frontiers of conventional wisdom. The contrast can be stunning. *Sleeping with Sophia* seeks to give poetic voice to some of the identifiable themes that characterize this emerging consciousness.

The archetype of the Feminine, referred to by Dr. Jung as *anima*, meaning *soul*, has awakened our collective imaginations to the many possibilities of soulfulness, especially in terms of human development. One hears new terms and expressions in the public domain that had hardly any currency at all a few decades ago. A short list would include splendid idioms such as: heart-work, soul-work, breath-work, Gaia, world-soul, sustainability, social justice, sacred sexuality, awakening, embodied awareness, grounding, earthing, birthing, intersubjectivity, unity consciousness, interconnection, hook-up, transpersonal, felt-sense, think globally-act locally, and so on. All of which articulate a very necessary shift away from ego-centric, greed-based consciousness to more evolved forms of egalitarian, Earth-centric, globally conscious values that are only now becoming recognizable.

For example, the concept of Embodiment, as it is used today, does not just refer to the human body but to our bond with the Earth as a living system of which we humans, other creatures, plants, the moon—all things that are *of* Earth—exist as integral parts of an interdependent wholeness. Our self-centered preoccupations become exposed as symptoms of our immaturity as individuals and as a species. Embodiment in this context alludes to a depth of soulfulness and full-heartedness that honors the innate intelligence of the Life Force animating all bodies. Indeed, the verb "animate" derives from the Latin cognate *anima*, equating life with soul. Thus, the gentle reader will find poems in this book that address not only the awakening of our human potential but also the 'growing pains' of our struggles with personal development and collective evolution.

Sophianic Wisdom is associated with the archetypal Feminine because of its emphasis on Eros rather than Logos and immanence rather than transcendence. This emerging consciousness expands our minds and opens our hearts regarding the most pressing issues that threaten Life on Earth. It seems that only when we allow our hearts to open will we *care* enough to intercede on our own behalf and grow ourselves into the potential human. *This* is Sophia, the Wisdom that is asleep within us that is now awakening. *This* is the Sophia with whom we are becoming intimate.

We currently find ourselves in the vortex of the most complex planetary dilemma in human history, where, consciously or unconsciously, we are actively or passively making decisions that not only affect the fate of our own species but the continued existence or extinction of countless other species as well. The existential wall we currently face evokes the stern admonition that we must *mature as a species or risk our demise*. Indeed, various aspects of this realization resound throughout *Sleeping with Sophia*.

As a man writing about women and the archetypal Feminine, my aesthetic temperament has had to be especially sensitive and responsive to the fact that the rise in the status and empowerment of women globally has increasingly brought into our collective awareness the historic abuses and excesses committed by patriarchy—not to be confused with the archetypal Masculine, which is an entirely different topic. In *Sleeping with Sophia* it has been important to me as a poet and as a man to allow these issues to influence my art. Resisting that influence eventually proved unsustainable for me on many levels. I felt it increasingly unwise, un-Sophianic, to politely ignore the ensconced planet-imperiling idolatry of greed and violence perpetuated, oftentimes under the banner of righteousness.

On a more stimulating note, it will perhaps come as no surprise that the theme of Eros does indeed run throughout *Sleeping with Sophia*. From my point of view, Eros describes the Life Force as we experience it in our bodies, in Nature and very importantly in the relationships we have with each other and our surroundings. The rise of the Feminine addresses the crucial need for large-scale 'unity consciousness' that subsumes motifs of collaboration, consensus, oneness in the face of diversity, the web of Life and an Earth-centric perspective that expands our Awakening to its broadest limits. Of course, much of this process requires becoming liberated from the old mindset that created the problems and rapidly learning instead to embrace a new 'heartset' capable of awakening not only a new orientation for our minds but also developing *calmer, gentler* minds in service of Life, rather than the usual deluded plots of self-aggrandizement that characterize so much of our personal and collective histories.

In my view, any worthwhile lingering over the topic of Eros must necessarily serve up heaping helpings of the soul's alchemy as expressed in the dazzling kaleidoscope of Love—especially when it comes to deeply caring and passionate expressions of Love. This entire book can readily be seen as a collection of love poems. I have had to be rather insistent with myself not to short-change the ripe area of Eros in *Sleeping with Sophia*.

My observation is that modern men and women often arrive in adulthood with various levels of emotional wounds and insecurities, sometimes compounded by trance-like mindsets of social privilege or social disadvantage. Many of us have to clear these hurtles, sometimes quite painfully, by developing emotional intelligence grounded in self-awareness. In our often insular, fast-paced and rather crazed Western societies, few people are left unscathed. Nonetheless, I *whole-heartedly* believe that relationships, especially intimate ones, have now become the egalitarian frontier for Awakening. Which is to say that by its very nature an intimate relationship provides us with an intense, and thus effective, crucible for becoming the possible human. With all of this in mind, the theme of Eros plays an essential role in *Sleeping with Sophia*.

These poems are about our struggle for Liberation. Some emphasize the inner journey, shared, as it were, with our inner-deity, in order to provide a dialogue with that depth in us that might otherwise remain naggingly unconscious. Other poems explore a particular form of ecstatic embodiment I call *sacred creaturehood*—that un-self-conscious state of awareness referred to as *élan vital* by the Romantic poets. I view an embodied form of Awakening as the indispensable ingredient in the process of soul-making in the Keatsian sense because Awakening itself is predicated upon the soul's success at attaining its fullest and most thorough measure of embodiment (by definition, the soul's incarnational assignment).

In our modernity we seem to be working our way through a rather thoroughgoing, madcap stage of cerebral development that impels us to dwell too much in our heads. This usually leads to a fractured state of disembodiment, psychological dissociation, disconnection with Earth and, all-to-often, a shocking absence of the type of Wisdom that Buddhists refer to as *bodhichitta*—the Big Mind and Big Heart needed to grow us out of our addiction to materialism and ego-centrism. One way to cultivate this type of Awakening is to revive the Indigenous Archetype inside ourselves that is capable of rooting our hearts and minds into our own interior ground of Being—a latency we have actually grown to revere, at least somewhat, as we familiarize ourselves with the state of Nature in which Original Peoples have lived . . . and still do live, where they manage to cling to survival despite the near certitude of extinction or assimilation. Indigenous mythical consciousness wends its way into some of these poems, as does the Buddhist concept of *adi-budhi*, the indwelling Buddha Nature that potentiates all sentient beings with the innate capacity for becoming Buddhas or Awakened Ones.

Being raised Catholic, I had the good fortune to be indelibly marked for life by the mystical codes of the Sacred Heart and the Sacred Feminine in the form of Mary. So very deeply rooted in me are these influences, they might as well have been genetically grafted into my DNA at birth. These inner-sources have contributed powerfully to my conviction that the shifts in consciousness I write about do indeed have supremely unifying, sacralizing effects that open the way for genuine Liberation.

The global rise of the Feminine is more than just a vision of an unfolding reality. It is also that singular Necessity that can transform our species. If this perception is even partially true, then we might all begin to envision the ways in which the ascendance of the Feminine might rapidly change our entire worldview as well as our life circumstances. Surely such a hope deserves a cornucopia of poetry, much less this very humble offering.

Lastly, I want to beg a technical indulgence. You will not find commas at the end of any of these poetic lines where you might ordinarily expect to find them. This intentional omission serves as a poetic device. Years ago the poet Fran Quinn drilled it into me that lineation actually does mean something in poetry beside window-dressing. In this case, it means that the line ends precisely where it does for the deliberate effect it will have on the reading of it and the next line. The end of the line thus signals a caesura (a breath-point or slight pause). Because the poems were composed to be read aloud, not just read silently, the lineation and punctuation serve to guide the reading cadence.

By the way, if you really enjoy these poems, please by all means, allow yourself to be titillated by reading them to your beloved. And if, by chance, you discover yourself feeling a wee bit subversive in the process, then smile to yourself knowing that your intuition is already guiding you into the playful mysteries of Sophia.

TABLE OF CONTENTS

Woman	1

I

Memory of an Afghan Woman	5
Purely of Herself	7
Songs of Sophia	8
Flicker of Moonlight	10
On the Hidden Horizon	12
The Body Enclosing My Body	13
Theatre of Spring	14
The Leap	15
Women on the Shore	16
Difunta Correa	17
My Daughters	21
In the News: Banaz Mahmod	23
Intimations of Woman	27

II

Carrie Allen McCray	31
Immaculate	33
Hard Lake	35
Friction of Heaven and Earth	37
Between Walls	38
The Remote	40
Bonedeep	42

Snake River	44
The Morning After	45
Talk	47
The Tao of Upheaval	48
Our Best Days	49
This Silence	50
This Song	51

III

Liquid Light	55
Daughter of Kali	57
Gate of Indi	59
Vierge Noire du Pilier	60
When She Was Lighthearted	63
Into the Light	65
Descent	67
Into the Silence	69
Passing	71
The Mind Turns Back	73
Dove Cottage	75
Sacred Hearts	77
Why I Must Feel Her Deeply Now	80
Into the Unknown Sea	82

IV

Stay the Long Night	87
The Empty Beach	89
A Suite of Creature Songs	91

Motionless Wings	93
Secret Attraction	95
Hieros Gamos under the Moon	97
The Art of Eating Grapes	99
Launched into the Infinite Years	101
Tea with Neruda	103
Peace of Heart	105
Proposal	107
In a Circle of Women	111
Acknowledgements	113

WOMAN

*Dedicated to the Sacred Feminine in All Women
and Its Seed in All Men*

With my feet bare I return to her, though
it does not suffice to speak only of roots
or ocean depths or even kinships and blood.
For when I seek my passage through her
or at my wisest, when I read her currents
as might a river steward, her dark origin and
womb of night enfold me in her mystery.

I bear her mystery in me like a deeply planted
seed, needing only to be reached by water.
Yet, after the rains have soaked into my body
dissolving the edges of my ancient crystals
I still find that the spirit of woman raises
or lowers her veil according to her season
and her seed in me sprouts beyond reason.

I

*Beloved, you are my sister, you are my daughter,
you are my face; you are me.*
—Toni Morrison

Photo by Omar Sobhani, Thomson-Reuters

MEMORY OF AN AFGHAN WOMAN

Outskirts of Amritsar, near the Pakistan border

My memory has its own film version:

I'm loitering at the café. The air reeks of burnt dung and diesel fumes. Sometimes there's a close-up of the cup, barely touching my lips like a hushing finger. Then my view snaps to the shot of the lone Afghan woman, draped in black. The frame tilts, and the visual gravity slides towards her. On cue, a cart topples, and its load of calabash smashes to pieces. Then there's the wide-angle shot of people staring at her, whispering behind their hands, as men in turbans push through on their way to the temple.

I don't know why the film sticks in places
or why I can't make it through the opening scene
without getting snagged in the acacia near my table.
In the film version, she's so close
I can almost touch her. Now, I wonder if that's true.

On the cutting room floor, sometimes there's a lioness
a few contrived images of a caravan
a huddle of starving refugees, and the scene where the woman
gets smeared with what looks like camel shit.

I don't know why I am the only one left transfixed
or why
in the little window of her hijab, I can see her eyes
catching fire, clouds roiling and bursting open
light streaming through and birds returning
as the storm of her life looks the other way
or why
those same eyes stab deeply into me
with the blade of a world, where I am too
foreign to ever really get the full picture.

A journalist notices I've become a still life.
He sees where I'm looking, and mutters:
Yes, that one.
She's one of the women
held captive and raped
for years on end by the Taliban.
    Oh, good Lord, you're spilling your tea.

In the closing scene, sometimes the café sparrows twitter
and fly off with slender threads or bits of straw
but before she turns away, her eyes harden
into sovereign metal, and no call rings out for the final
    cut, or if there is one, I never hear it.

PURELY OF HERSELF

No one knows
how I have struggled to become simple
as I aspire
to wade amidst the colors of the day
and be content
when radiance
sloughs off
being named.

For I would have myself be humble
and spend whole days
simply watching with my heart
so that when a woman speaks
     when my love speaks
I could be a mirror
she would *wish* to stand before
to see something
that did not   come   from me
but a glow, a tint, a flare, a firmness
that could only be *her* gift
so thoroughly received
simply being there
in that moment
she would taste *purely of herself*
without knowing how it happened
only knowing that it did.

SONGS OF SOPHIA

Singing in the blood
resounding in caves and bones
beyond self-imposing edges

chanted over centuries for the heresies
of being woman
with lunar tides and juicy womb

spilling life's lyrics with the
splendor of each season's drama.
Heard amid weeping children

clutching crimson thorns
of households during Sunday
salons in high-ceiling rooms with bright

bay windows and sun-faded seats
and in grottos under leaky floors
that cover perpetually-rising water.

Heard in streambeds of streets that flood
underworld chambers lost in time.
Heard in the fractured moments of

midlife's pause, pulsing in her ears—
a time to air the furnishings
with wizened winds across narrow stretches

between the seen and unseen
gathering and tugging the skin
seeping into every pore

quenching each brazen cell.
Her wild daughters
dance in the moon's garden

while singing heart sutras
saints scarcely recognize
till scorched by stars and candles.

Sophia with unexpected fire
sets wet wood ablaze
reducing rooftops to cinders.

Spread a banquet at her feet
for the onyx woman rises
oozing honey where she stands.

FLICKER OF MOONLIGHT

Some part of me knows moonlight
is merely flickering in your eyes
and that this moment is but a moment
vulnerable as any other.

My thoughts alone
cannot begin to fathom this emptiness
that aches to drink you in
nor how darkness can be illuminated
by the mere flicker of love's light
the way fireworks kindle a starless sky
or the way a candle's flame reassures
an entire household after a storm.

I've caught the moon's minions
conspiring with primal darkness
to deliver it from oblivion
    because
something is more alive and more playful
in your eyes than anywhere else
and I feel it quickening my body
with the gift that can come only through you
as if my life and the entire world
sought existence only to behold
these moments of love
and whatever it is in me that wants
to be separated or clenched or armored
    disappears
and whatever it is that feels playfully alive
    opens

like petals in the sun's first light
in that moment of awakening
when the dove's cry
finally, unexpectedly, pierces the heart
and tears of awe quench the blazing
intercourse of heaven and earth.

ON THE HIDDEN HORIZON

the long blind walk
to the water's edge
waiting for the moon
to emerge from the black sea
a presence like water
felt
though not yet seen

my bare feet are chilled
by waves of frothy tongues
and
I don't know where she is
or where she's not
or even what to call her
except I feel her moving
in the starless night
like a vast endless woman
made of sand, wind, water
and everything that crests
and falls, the heartbeat of tides
of seasons, of orbits
in a sky full of novas
and collapsing light

then in a sudden hush
the world holds its
breath, as her orb appears
and we stand together
stripped bare of everything
except each other

THE BODY ENCLOSING MY BODY

The dark mood of midnight
begins to lighten
as I notice a lamppost
flecked with faint leaves
now pendulous
as sculpted jade
dripping dew. The consoling fog
laden with the marshy spoor of the harbor
quakes as a foghorn bellows.

From my balcony over the street
my heart is stabbed with longing
as I watch a young couple strolling hand-in-hand
pouring out their hearts
in a huddled oneness.

The lamp casts its corona on their union
a scene intoxicating, somehow almost legendary.
I find an accusation there, something I am missing
in the blur, that wants to be seen
in the silhouette of this oak-leaf bough
in the texture of its bark and
in the grayscale of the curly moss.

A moist hand reaches out
from the vast black ocean
and finds my hand, and I feel her
steadfast body enclosing my body
as the lovers pass, whispering innocently.

THEATRE OF SPRING

In my play full of women
I'd cast you as Mary Magdalene
and there would be no script
that would have you bow down
or lower your gaze

because when your craving
embraces mine, our bodies
weave myths out of moonbeams
more dazzling
and more dangerous

than the heathen millennia
spent in bloodied trenches
beneath the heedless gods
floating like tinsel virgins
above spring's
blossoming riot.

THE LEAP

A sandbar, born a few weeks ago
of an autumn storm, extends its languid arm
out into the ocean.

Something neon-green moves
in sharp contrast on its distant tip.
A runner rounds the point
as the swift tide fills the inlet
wide and deep
by the time she reaches it.

I watch her leap like a dancer
into the arms of the wind, her forefoot
making a bright splash. Her face flushes
as she lets out a squeal of glee—the precious
irrepressibly free and wild exuberance
of her deep-down animal passion!
She smiles to herself, perhaps
because she sees me spellbound.

As her form recedes along the water's edge
I feel I've glimpsed an image of her soul
risking everything to run on its own ground.

An hour later, I see her walking serenely
holding hands with another woman, lovingly
and I wonder
what other inlets she's had to leap.
In amazement at myself, I feel a hand
clutch my heart, hoping she landed then also
with an equally joyful, blazing splash.

WOMEN ON THE SHORE

"Of course the starfish must go back!"
Your hands held out a possibility, although
your face held an agony, immense as the galaxy
of gasping starfish, embedded in the sky's
mirror—constellations drowning in air
like washed-up survivors of an unseen wreck.

I wonder if there is some secret pheromone
that summons women, some inner ear for little cries
because women gathered on the shore
as though guided by a call or a twitch felt
a beckoning in their nature
that simply could not be suppressed.

Without a word, they spread like fingers
of a single hand, cradling starfish to the sea.
A girl beside her mother wept
as if the cold creatures were her loved ones.

Double-dogged as man and skeptic
I doubted what they did, however noble its intent.
Who knows the ways of starfish?
This beach might be the bone yard of ancestors.

Yet, this day taught me to trust
the mystery of hope these women held.
Their hearts, trembling, overflowing, knew
only one Life and the need to care for it.

LA DIFUNTA CORREA

Photo by Thomas Locke Hobbs of shrine site in Argentina

Maria Antonia Deolinda Correa's husband was abducted from his family by militant partisans to fight in their civil war in Argentina. When Deolinda received word that her husband had taken ill and abandoned by the militia, she set off with her baby to find him. During the journey, however, she died of dehydration in the arid outback of Patagonia. Her dead body was found by shepherds. Miraculously, her child was still alive, nursing at her breast. Her grave soon became a pilgrim site. The dark-skinned mother with her black hair and peasant's red dress has risen as a popular saint, a Black Madonna of the people with overtones of Mary Magdalene, inspiring the citizens of Patagonia with hope for their own survival and renewing their belief in miracles. These days, her shrines abound in the countryside and are often crowded with offerings of water bottles, prayers on folded paper, candles and even highly valued soccer shoes. A town called Vallecito has formed around her burial site, consisting of 17 votive chapels and pilgrim accommodations. During Easter and All-Souls' Day, crowds of 200,000 come from all over South America to venerate her and to pray for her strength.

Well, my son, you're off
to Patagonia . . . of all places.
How I envy you!
I can almost feel the urgent call
of wilderness
tugging at your 19 year-old body
with promises of manhood.
On your expedition, should you embrace
new loves, let them be Earth & Woman
for a man has no greater need
than to be cracked open by them
and our hearts increased by
their wondrous and luscious
scents, skin, curves, textures
coloring, moods, cycles and desires.
At every turn, I pray you
tread lightly
and respect their autonomy.
May you feel in your cells
how you are wrought of
their elements and seasons.
May you hear *their*
hearts beating in your chest.
May you love
what they have already given you
at times at great expense.
I know the fears you carry
for I have had my share of years
overshadowed by circling birds
and felt the cold hand
of dread clench my gut.
Even now I feel it.

We men are sucking Earth dry
gorging at her lovely breasts
like grown-up infants
consuming everything in sight
then spewing our effluent
as if we were invulnerable
little gods
poisoning Earth's body
conscripting ourselves as men
the way Deolinda Correa's husband
became one of *The Disappeared*
stolen from his home
to wage war in Argentina.
So many men, far gone in madness
far gone in greed
seeking to possess and subdue
Earth & Woman
as if they were the chattel
and whore of every whim.

Now, throughout Patagonia
the winds weep for the death of
Deolinda Correa
whose soul they recognize
as their own.
Up from their living soil
she rises as a saint.
Her baby, alive at her breast
is *their* future!
The Madonna of Patagonia
emerges no less for you, my son

in the parched, pure wilderness of your manhood.
The heart of the People has bloomed
with pilgrim offerings
for the People's saint.

I pray this dark woman dressed in red
La Difunta Correa
preserve the innate goodness
I see in you and protect you
from the maladies of disembodied men
so that in your heart you always know
what it does
and does *not* mean to be a man.

MY DAUGHTERS

For Germaine and Rosalind

Listen, my daughters, as your father
so often has, to the heart-piercing whales—
their songs, the sonorous tidings
of a thousand exiled violins
in an ocean of tears.
Like us, they would surely drown
were it not for the ascent
and the bursting through—
light and freeing, yet
fleeting.

In the stillness of breath
before you were born, life
among the whales was
the only type of love I had ever known
collecting and bulging in distant bays
visited by humpbacks and minkes, until
suddenly, one by one, you emerged
like mermaids on my shore.

The ocean of your eyes
flooded my world
and awakened the love
this man could learn
only from his children.

All my sacred yearnings
and celebrated wounds
turned into far-fetched schemes

falling uselessly from my hands
whenever I held you.

Thus amid the heart-quake
of caring for you
a strong and true
joy and goodness arrived
and I realized
for the first time
what love is.

London, UK police file photo

IN THE NEWS: BANAZ MAHMOD

    Banaz Mahmod, beautiful 20 year-old, strangled, buried in the backyard. . . . Get this, her father and uncle were found guilty of murdering her.
    OK, that's worth getting pissed-off about. What did she ever do to them?
    Don't know yet . . . the paper says they're Kurdish . . . moved to England nine years ago . . . her father beat her for using hairspray.
    And this led to her own family killing her . . . because of what, she made herself at home where she was living?
    Something like that . . . the paper says, at first the father convinced the brother to kill her, but he couldn't finish her off, so they hired someone else to do it.
    Let me get this straight, these are not psychos . . .

They're calling it an "honor killing" . . . the men said she brought shame on them . . . she fell in love with a guy who wasn't from their village . . . so . . . badabing . . .

That's not in the least bit funny.

No, but these guys have dedicated their lives to some theocratic old-world sense of honor, so they have to be this way or else they'd be crossing God.

So you're saying exactly what, that these fundamentalist killers are just God's gangstas? No, try this on instead, it's the same shit men have been doing to women for centuries . . . burn a woman alive when she becomes too holy or too emotional, make her into either a virgin or a whore, so they can beat her, rape her . . . reduce her to a dehumanized object, and then . . . well, and then, I guess you can rationalize doing whatever you want to her.

Hmm . . . could be . . . the paper says they're investigating more than 100 of these honor killings . . . in Britain alone. Listen to this, "Years of abuse were compounded by police officers who refused to believe her and dismissed her cries for help."

Please tell me those officers weren't women . . . I don't believe other women would have ignored her.

Don't be so sure . . . women buy into it, they become good daughters of the patriarchy and can't help circumcising each other.

What?!

Maasai women use razor blades on each other . . . men aren't doing that . . . the women are doing that to each other.

Except that a man can still get off after he's circumcised . . . the woman is left sexually mutilated and numb . . . and what do you suppose drove them to become a tribe of neutered women in the first place?

But that's my point, she's being neutered by her own gender, so her sexuality won't cause any trouble . . . or God-forbid, that she have too much pleasure.

Thanks for that, but there's more to it . . . men want to be able to take sex . . . like it shows weakness for them to have any feelings . . . Except for lust and rage . . .

Are you saying men are inherently afraid of women?

I'm saying they fear their own inner feminine . . . and when they can dominate women it's like disconnecting from that part in themselves.

Are you kidding me? I know plenty of soft men . . . metrosexuals, even . . . and women just adore them.

It's the virgin or whore ultimatum all over again . . . the man is hung out to dry in his logos, like an ambulatory cerebrum made out of erectile tissue . . . and has to either capitulate to women or dominate them . . . anything to avoid having depth and range of authentic feelings . . . and when he can't beat a woman, literally it seems, sometimes he'll just give up and join her.

But then she ends up with the soft semblance of a man who can't run off a burglar or stand up for himself . . . or her.

Better that than ending up like Banaz Mahmod, murdered by her own father who is convinced he's defending the Supreme Being's alpha-male reputation.

Oh, I see where this is going . . . so if the Supreme Being were a *woman*, we'd have a better crop of men with much improved attitudes? OK, I'll go along with it . . . as long as She makes Banaz's father reincarnate as a woman . . . from their native village and have to face . . . OK, I guess the superior female God would never tolerate the eye-for-an-eye thing.

It's so tidy, isn't it, when you treat everything in life like it's a thought problem. No heart-rending sorrow, no moral outrage, even though Banaz's murder is a blazing example of the violence women have suffered at the hands of men for eons. Where's the public outcry, where's the fierce heart wailing? Banaz's life has been snuffed out! We should be howling! But you're right . . . if we had been brought up with something more balanced, like a Mother-Father deity, then perhaps every single person who saw Banaz's picture and heard her story would be moved to tears, and the hearts of men might crack open . . . that would be a start at least.

I've heard you say this before . . . the most ancient view of God was the Mother God, like in Africa, or the Mother-Father God, like in India. So, you're saying it's time to bring back the Mother?

Why not? We need the Mother right about now to straighten out this mess . . . I doubt she meant for the patriarchy to run amuck, warring till millions are dead and Nature desecrated to the point of annihilation!

Then, let me ask you this—if we're going to project Father *and* Mother onto God, then why not a Man-Woman androgyny onto ourselves?

We don't have to project that, my love, that's the way we actually are.

Ergo, the soft male?

No more than we have to have patriarchal women . . . it's all a question of balance.

That's a stretch. My inner feminine seems to be on an extended holiday.

Look, women want men who are safe to be around, that's all, and the only way that can happen is for men to derive their strength from love.

Instead of love of strength, strength from love?

They can use their strength to be towering mountains of love! Like all the gentle-hearted men we have loved throughout history, like Gandhi and the Dalai Lama . . .

And men want what, wonderwoman?

I hope not, or else they tend to get stuck in the never-never land of the lost boys, when what the world desperately needs right now is mature men of great conscience and compassion. I think most men really want that for themselves . . .

Hmm . . . you're full of surprises. I'm always learning something from you.

Just look at Banaz . . . just look at her photo.

My love, are you crying?

And what about you? Doesn't her death hurt your heart . . . even a little?

INTIMATIONS OF WOMAN

For her beauty alone, I would adore her, and when her body
        sprawls next to mine
I realize how supremely I love woman's natural state. In truth
        I find her intimations
everywhere, in all things natural and free-flowing.
        I see her in the curve
of cresting waves, in the waistline of meandering streams
        slanty roofs
with their bowed ridges, arched doorways, and without fail
        I find her décolletage
in every bowl of peaches! I hear her in the roundy wells
        and the canyons birthing
echoes, and no less in the arias of brooks, birdsong of every kind
        and in the winds haunting my eaves.
Is there any place in Nature
        her scent is not? In leaf-mold, rusty blood, the exhale
of salty marsh
        or the cornucopia of herbs, fruits, forests, and the billion-
fold perfumes of flowers?
        Her dance undulates
in all things round, wavy, cascading, turning, lilting, soaring
        and pulsating.
Yet, even more as I grow older and can open more fully to her
        I find her
rooted in the living soil, in willows, oak limbs, roiling fields
        palm fronds
cinnamon ferns, almond eyes, thick lips—puffy red lips that shout
        across crowded streets
"I bear the labia you seek!
        Round hips
that sway and pump on promontory thighs of every hue.

      I see her in the mud
oozing rainbows, and in vast sprawling seas under the
          pregnancy of clouds.
All the heavens in my telescope reveal textures of her glory
          spiraling to the very edges
          of the void she yearns to fill
          and always, always
                when I see the moon
                I feel she's watching
                like a lover
                whose face has many phases
                yet whose constancy
                my soul has never doubted.

                I have a soul . . . this I know
                because her secrets run too deep
                and far for all but souls to hear.
                Listen, she's whispering now . . .

II

The moment of change is the only poem.
—Adrianne Rich

Provided by Ms. McCray

CARRIE ALLEN McCRAY

Her face had that light I love to see
when the residue of all of life's clutter
has been metabolized so near to completion
a transparency takes hold, like a poem
that is finally as finished
as it's ever going to be.
Her sweet smile was that way too, only
with a slight tilt that made me wonder
if there were stories hidden in it
that had not been fully told.

I can tell you this much: when she read
her poetic chronicles, I felt the room swell
with the shades of civil rights marchers

and freedom riders, gathering to hear
her heart make its own confessions

as though these long dead friends
still craved to reflect on what they'd learned
and what must never be forgotten.

Finally, the poetry books closed and her naked
voice wended through the images
of visiting a Confederate General's grave
a slaveholder
known only as "my mother's father."

Standing there before his headstone
she reached into their blood
and felt her heart open.

"I went because
I found out my grandfather
had sent my mother to college."

Carrie Allen McCray knew
in that moment
her mother's father might have
actually loved them.

IMMACULATE

Take, for example, the marvel of the office
carpet, when assayed by her discerning eye:
the compressed curls of twirled nylon in
randomized waves, with the merest hint of
subdued chaos, manufactured to miraculous
tolerances by industrial-strength gods. The
pinstripes in her suit could flare fire when
tilted at an angle, as if some secret device
sent its current through her threads.
Her shoes of supple python, her perfect lips
and eyes, her hair like a show horse's mane.
Nowhere in her immaculate order is tone mis
cued or voice raised

    no, not ever, ever

    a single trace

    of her liquored-up

father

    storming in

    slamming her mother

    like a beer can against the wall

kicking her knocked out body

    straddling her

    like a colossus

    firing his curses like a gun.

She learned the blessings of quietness
    and to make it pass for love.
She saw in the recesses of her mother's eyes
    a blade, buried to the hilt, severing
    her roots.
Today, in this high-rise building
business is bursting at the seams.
Boxes are piled and out of place, like
the scatter of sweaty shirts, like

      dishes overnight in the sink, like
      eggs still in their henhouse cribs, like
      the insanity of a shaking fist.
      The mortifying flight to neighbors' homes
      in her blood-stained hand-me-downs
      old boys hooting in the county lock-up
      then back at the mill before the horn
      house set straight, the welcome-home meal
      ending with the sullen, muted exile
      into the shade of the suicide tree.

She entrusted the boxes to someone on her staff
    though uncertain to exactly whom.
After all, she spent the morning in sessions
    a schedule, tight as the textiles she adores.
When she returns wearing a pair of jeans
    underlings scramble like children
    to prevent *her* from doing *their* chores.
    She certainly has better things to do
than carry boxes, which was
    after all, delegated to you . . . or was it you?
Of course, her point stabs home.
    With good help so hard to find
    the only one you can
    ever really count on
    is none other than yourself.

HARD LAKE

A chilled wind, down from the snowy ridges
litters the lake with cup-sized waves
blank as doll's eyes
floating silently

as the day drains away. The rising moon
scatters a few bright coins
onto the lake's eyelids.
A young woman on the shore shudders
and blinks
as if to shake free.

She has come to fling herself
upon the lake's skin
and let oblivious arms rise up
and have their way.

Her mother finally ran her off. Now
it seems she'd turn out just like her
a string of feckless men
drawn into her desert
misled by her moist lips.

The girl's hands drift
down onto her belly
as her body remembers
its wordless weight.

She watches the sunset
dust its rouge of alpenglow

on the cheeks of the distant Sierras.
Without knowing why
she lifts a smooth, round stone
and with hands now trembling
wets it
with unexpected tears.

Tucking it underneath her thumb
she will rub it all the way home
till it feels like newborn skin.

FRICTION OF HEAVEN AND EARTH

Which of the deities
in the abode of luminous minds
did you rail against
when your love died?

Sentimental and petulant
did you brood for days on end
wringing each one's neck
and cursing their names?

Did the villains in your drama
admit their guilt
or did your sour breath whip
like a gale across their pale faces?

At first, when you learned
about dying, those same reproved
deities stewed in their wisdoms
and turned their faces from you.

Yet, slyly, in their hearts
they hid their secret envy
each time death taught you
to lay your body down.

BETWEEN WALLS

Amelia Island, Florida

I walk through a clutter of shells
   churned by the receding tide—shards
being ground to sand—broken sand-dollars
   the cutting edge of razor clams
and a lone, perfect angel wing.

I pick up the spiraling top
   of a bull's-eye. It is a labyrinth
worth keeping. A whelk, filigreed
   with worm holes.
Oyster shells turned gray—not one still has its shine.

A skate's purse, a scallop's hinge
   millions of minute coquina
that crunch under foot. Mostly
   there are clamshells, carved by worms
fading pink . . . on their way

to turning black. A pristine shore
   without a speck of human litter. At the edge
of the tide-line, a million yards of dredged sand
   form a bunker shaped by bulldozers, fortifying
the first line of defense in the ongoing war

against Nature, to protect the wall of condominiums
   that stretches all the way to the Nature Preserve
at the island's tip. Ahead, there is another wall
   a brown wall, like a dingy curtain draped
over the beach in front of me.

As I walk into it, I am repulsed by a stench
    I can trace to the nearby pulp mill.
Are we the species that fouls its own nest, perhaps
    beyond repair? I suppose, over time
even the worst of our poisons revert to Nature.

Walking between these walls, I think
    of Boethius in his cell awaiting execution.
I wonder what consolations I might contrive, when
    in the corner of my eye, a plover gulps a tiny crab
just as a pelican plops with a great splash, head first

as if the sound were the kerplunk of a Basho poem.
    I walk away, once again entranced
back to being the same creature I was before
    fascinated by all the washed-up shells
lulled by the incessant chorus of tranquil waves.

THE REMOTE

the news tonight runs old Katrina footage
of riots, a few black guys looting
then reports of a tsunami and
footage of brown bodies
being bulldozed
        while I'm cooking dinner

there they go
        brown bodies tumbling
in front of a massive blade
heaped into massive gravesites
while I'm stranded alone at the stove
stirring a pot
without the remote nearby
just then, in a flash, before my eyes
an IED tears through a Hum-V
and I see Marines blown apart

just think, I say to myself
actual people are being killed on my TV
actual people

and I remember the footage of people jumping
to their deaths from the Twin Towers

and I can almost smell the smoke
oh shit, sorry, it's my food burning

out of nowhere
it just overwhelms me

those camouflaged soldiers are *my* people
those black people are *my* people
and the brown bodies being bulldozed

those are *my* people! *My people!!*   What if
I allow myself to really feel this . . . to feel
even in my limited way
the world's pain, the Earth's pain
the tumbling bodies, the fish-kills, the oily birds . . .
just for one minute?

Already I can feel the rising oceans
trying to pour through me
their waves, glutted with corporate criminals
getting away with murder.
How glibly they plunder the world
laying low the proverbial *least of these*
without the slightest care

and I, standing there
craven and alone
never anticipated
just how susceptible I would feel
without that bloody remote   control.

BONEDEEP

Whenever two are gathered
in the name of love
bonedeep is deep enough
to shatter bones—
the muzzle velocity of blame
the bullet holes of contempt
the body-count of betrayals.
Who knew hidden fears
could go on such a rampage?

Only gradually
did pain teach us
to outgrow the drug of self-importance
and the rush of righteousness
and instead
to allow love's patience
to burrow so deeply into our bones
that nothing
nothing can remove it.

Remember the time
when you tripped over
that buried chunk of rose quartz
in the middle of our path?
"At last!" you cried
the prized heartrock
you were so determined to own.
You dug at its edges with a broken stick
but it would not budge.

When you saw how tightly
the tree's roots gripped it
you smeared your face with tears
and sat
silently   in the summer shade.

                                Down by the stream
wasn't it a muddy stone, brown as dung
you heard weeping
    loud enough to tremble your legs and arms?

We stayed there so long
the path was lost in darkness
and the few words left for us
were the ones that gripped our hearts
      because they went bonedeep.

SNAKE RIVER

Jackson Hole, Wyoming

The riverbed is strewn with palm-size granite
    smooth as cheeks under the August moon.
Four women walking along the edge
    have this day heard a hidden eagle
and seen a moose nurse her calf.

Near the water's edge, dusty stones wobble
    under their feet as the women crouch
and peer through the river's skin for the wet
    roundness each yearns to hold, like
a shining infant for the moon's blessing.

Their eyes seek hints of the new life
    that can only catch fire in water.
Their hands have no urge to throw stones
    as men's hands do

    only to hold
    and to feel

    the way water
patiently wears the mightiest sediments
    into the sands that fly at all hours.

THE MORNING AFTER

At dawn, your flailing arm
like a Zen master's stick
smacked me wide awake
and for the first time, the glad animal
in me beheld the slumbering creature
beside me as if for the first time.
My newborn senses delighted
in your pastures of pores
your fields of brazen follicles
with their earthy tang of fern and moss.
Like an explorer on a new frontier
I found the native beauty
of your body a natural wonder.
Your moist, textured skin
made me more simple-minded
than a wordless poet.

No fantasy could offer
the simple pleasures I found
admiring the creases of your mouth
or the little wine-spill
of a birthmark on your neck
somehow I had never noticed
till the curious creature in me
roused at last the primal man
whose awestruck hands now glissade
feather-light over your skin
inspired by the purring slipstream
of your breath, tracing the ridges
and valleys of your body as one might

dare touch the painterly peaks
and gessoed skin of the rarest art.

Suddenly, your eyes blink wide
and reach so deeply into me
I tremble
like a naked beggar
seen through to the core
by God in human form.

TALK

How is it we can speak about it
and even name it
without ever actually entering into
whatever it is?
It does not matter what *it* is
you might still get up
and walk across the room
and sit by the window.
Its source cannot be known
but felt, rushing through our veins.
Oh yes, we can share
the secrets of a thing that is
hidden and at the same time present
as the confluence of our great streams
forms an even mightier river
that we navigate with effort
till nothing remains unspoken
that might impede our flow.

We'd rather err
on the side of talking.
Although no words
could ring as true as your silent eyes
or express the passion of touching
or the fragrance of your hair.
Let us resolve to go on and on
touching each other
with ungloved hands
while digging in this soil
of honest talk.

THE TAO OF UPHEAVAL

How clearly I know these upheavals
for what they truly are.

How sudden and portentous they loom
like storm-clouds blackening the view

and then, just as suddenly, bursting open
calling me farther into my wounded heart.

Though my mind cringes and writhes
my heart yearns to expand, to embrace

and to contain all of it. And so it does
as I return from the surges of fear

and grief, undress myself, and slip into
silence, where peace brushes my skin

like love's warm and patient hand.
Then so clearly I see it as an act of grace

that today's illusions fell apart, as I dare
hope that sooner or later they all might.

OUR BEST DAYS

Today, there is no place
for doubt, no careless words
capable of keeping love from
soaking deep into my bones.

A woman's tenderness taught me
that of all the things that pass for love
possessions are the poorest
crumbling like clods of dirt
in my hungry hands
because I would gladly
forego a thousand fortunes
than lose this precious woman's

loving gaze, dripping its sweet
pomegranate into my veins
like an elixir, tingling with her
soul's secret alchemy, making
everything else seem a mere diversion
or a going astray.

In all this most beguiling world
only those beauties made of love
can rouse me from safe routines
into the fierce and feral passions
we risk sharing on our best days.

THIS SILENCE

Franklin, New Hampshire

This is a silence
I know better than anything else
and love better, not more, than anything else
a silence unbroken, as I emerge from sleep
at the 3:00AM clang of metal
piercing the absolute darkness
awakening aches of days of stillness.
The hall fills with shuffling feet.
The wood stove hisses.

The door breaches. Bundled people
step out onto the walkway, newly shoveled.
The meditation lodge a scant 30 footsteps
from the door: the pristine smell of snow
the thick, wool blanket bundling me
the muffling drifts slanting up the walls
—all these strains blend
with the deafening silence
into which I must immerse myself.

Inner sounds flood my ears
loud and chastening as God's voice, as I sit
on my meditation cushion, dangling
over the only chasm steep enough
and open enough
to shed whatever might die of silence
and lay bare whatever might be born of it.

THIS SONG

One day a man finally hears
his beloved speaking
without even for a moment
confusing her with someone else
without hearing echoes
of another time
another well-honed grievance
etched
so deeply into him
only the miracle of love
could possibly set him free.

In this moment, he allows
her voice to flow through him
as if it were made of music.
He feels her surging energy
pressing past the sift of meaning.
He reels with her precious heat
even amidst the mouthful of words
that had once clutched and clawed.

For in this moment, he lingers
over her words the way he might
a golden-throated bird, whose song
pours straight into his heart
into his veins, down into his bones
beyond the shadows of doubt
into the soul
that took birth for the sake of
this moment
and this very song

simply because it comes from her
simply because he has claimed love
instead of a little plot of importance.

In that moment the man glows
like the sun touching earth's horizon
piercing the woman's soul
that also took birth
for the sake of
this moment
and this very song.

III

It may be that the satisfaction I need depends on my going away, so that when I've gone and come back, I'll find it at home.
—Jalal ad-Din Rumi

Photo by author
Washwalla women in Mumbai, India

LIQUID LIGHT

Rishikesh, India

from the ashram's balcony, I see
the sky trembling in the dark west
as razor-slashes of light
rip through the indigo billows
obliterating the much sought
spectacle of sunset

all part of the mysterious, eternal *mela*[1]
put on by Herself (as we've come to call her)
in the guise of a night storm

the wind bangs loose a shutter
and it explodes into pieces

she knows all I can do is stay awake and pray
which is my wont
as her rain cascades from the ashram's roof
in a curtain of liquid light

source-seeking rills
on their way home to Ganga[2]
holy as pilgrims' prayer beads
holy, because she washes the sorrows
of this weary world onto leaves
down to roots, headlong to the Earth's heart
where even my most pathetic worries

---

[1] Mela (Hindi): annual Hindu festivals, often very colorful and wildly ecstatic, usually honoring a goddess or god, and often attracting tens of thousands of participants
[2] Ganga (Hindi): name of the holy river, anglicized as "Ganges;" the river itself is believed to be and worshipped as a living goddess.

resolve into a clay, to be molded
fired and then shattered into pieces
of sympathy for all suffering things
until clemency flows in my blood
to my soul-tendrils' farthest reaches
where the meekest Namaste of the poor
bursts my heart
into love poems

Photo by author
Muslim children in Veranassi, India

DAUGHTER OF KALI

Her untamed blood
    pulses fiercely
        with feral love.

Her body sways
    with ecstasy of itself
        dancing its own song.

Pubescent boys and girls
    have dreams tormented
        by her dancing body.

Do not be deceived
    by the dark honeycomb
        of her voice! For in *her*

lurks what is wild
    in women: the primal
        flesh-bearing woman

the woman who delivers
    her own babies
        with her own hands

who severs the umbilicus
    with teeth and nails and
        exalts the sacred ground

   of her quiet nest
        with musky plumes
              of the afterbirth

she buries under root-tips
        returning her womb
              to Earth, seeding

her sovereign soul
        deep in the marrow
              of every living woman.

GATE OF INDIA

Mumbai, India

Near the colossal Gate of India
stands the Taj Hotel
recently bombed
by Pakistani terrorists.
Police patrol the grounds of the Taj
holding the frontline
of its bruised opulence
against the encroachment
of Mumbai's squalor.

As I walk along the waterfront
a young mother follows me
with an infant on her hip
"Please, sir, I need milk powder.
Please, sir. . . . milk money. . . ."

Later, I meet her brother
a driver who makes a decent wage.
"Yes, she must be made to beg.
That child, he is a mistake she made."

Nearby, a blind man has no hands or feet.
They were burned off in a fire.
Each day I speak to him
and give him a few rupees.

I think he is mumbling his gratitude
but a Hindu passerby says
"That Baba, he prays . . .
             for *you!*"

Photo by author

VIERGE NOIRE DU PILIER

Black Madonna
Chartres Cathedral, France

Three women
immersed in a hushed chatter.
A fourth burly-looking woman sits nearby
eyes sealed, lips mumbling
fingers brooding over prayer beads.

Finally, the women gather their belongings and file out.
I've been distracted by them for so long
I feel compelled to stare.

The chatty ones genuflect in the aisle
then—incredibly—casually walk around the altar
and stand in the sanctum sanctorum before the Madonna.
The women lay their hands on the stone column
rosaries dangling, faces luminous.
At once, their fervor overwhelms me.
I watch them bless themselves and leave Her
reluctantly with backward glances.

Now, the burly-looking one takes her turn.
Embracing the column, her arms stretch
upwards, achingly, towards the Madonna.
I feel her yearning burrowing into me
even as my mind goes blank.

She kisses the pillar with fierce passion
her face mashing into the hard stone.

Unabashed in her fervency
she slowly backs away, eyes moist
trained on La Vierge Noire.
Alone now, I genuflect before the altar
walk around it, and step into the charged air
of intimacy. I too lay hands on the column.

Up close, I see the build-up of skin-oil
the lipstick and rouge coloring the pillar—

the centuries of this *affaire d'amour* with Her
suddenly, vivid and compelling clear
as Life itself.

I feel a bond
with my unexpected mentors.
I *must* surrender
I *must* embrace the pillar
and allow it to become my conduit.

A quiver spreads through my body.
Tears fill my eyes.
I let go and let Her in.
Something rigid falls away
and a vow pulses in my blood.

My heart smiles
tendering its secret
assured that in *this* moment
the real pilgrimage begins.

WHEN SHE WAS LIGHTHEARTED

or at least not quite so fretful
my mother'd sing, "Go tell Aunt Dina
the old gray goose is dead."
No sadness was in her voice
as though the song's meaning
sat waiting in the parlor
like an unexpected guest.

When I burned with rheumatic fever
she sang that song to me
and put ice to my lips. For days
her fingers raked my hair
as if her hands were possessed
by the memory of the hard pull of tines
or the cautious bend of a mended hoe.

Her top fingers were dyed yellow
from all the cigarette clutching, her eyes
dewy from the smoke hanging on her lips.
When I recovered, her perfunctory hugs
bolstered me like a brace for my next step.

By the time she lost her second son
the worst thing that could happen
seemed like it always would.
I could fall and smash my face.
She was sure of it. Then one day *she* did.
She stopped going to the beauty parlor.
What's the point, with a smashed face.

Years later, as she rocked my son to sleep she sang, "Fe fi fiddle-e-i-o, strumming on the ole banjo." Her body was at last where she always dreamed it should be.

INTO THE LIGHT

You loved to walk
the length of the island
from the lighthouse to the inlet.
Remember the sunlight
on winter's slate-flecked sea?
And on the beach
the jumbled reeds
of a thousand memories?

In spring, you'd crush wax myrtle
between your palms
and pronounce its odor
the essence of pure beach.
Remember the water's liquid gold
its hardest hue to hold
tremulous at sunset
the sky streaked pink and turquoise
melding in a seamless swirl?

All summer, the waves contended
like siblings
clashing with each other, making big sprays
with their cross-currents.
Don't they know
they are made of ocean?
Remember how the heat
shimmered on the sand?
Your broad hat and dad's long shirt
covering your freckles and pale skin—
all that to-do, and you still burned.

Autumn hurricanes ignored *our* roof
you said, because your father
my dear grandfather, PaPa
built his house of love.
The sign over the door
"Snug Harbor"
was all the proof we needed.

    Early this morning
    on your hospice bed
    mother, you heaved a sigh
    and now you are gone.
    Before my eyes, your body
    suddenly, visibly, deflated.
    I know your soul walked
    straight into the light.

If only I could have read a poem
like this to you, as you awaited death
if only I could have
reminded you of all the light you had known
what a living poem that would have been!

    Instead, just before you died
    I whispered, "Mom, you'll always
    be my best girl"
    and you whispered back
        "Don't let anyone know."

DESCENT

No one in his right mind
would dare descend
into the cold fire
at the bottom of grief
unless thrown down
bound and beaten.
No one would descend
that rough-hewn shaft
splaying the heart wide open.
No one would willingly
squeeze through
the death canal
headlong into the compost
of dejected memories.
No one would set his foot
a step closer to the dissolving
darkness, with only fingers for eyes
and only feet for feeling the way—
the giant thinker in him
riddled by bullets of ice.

Until, breathless, one day
it stops . . .
the descent stops.

The descent stops
because the heart finds its floor
in that cavern, in that dark hour
when stars
of pale phosphorus sediment

come into view, and darkness crumbles
itself into a living soil, and the frailest
faintest pulse of water
drips
from a lone, dangling, exposed root
twitching like God's finger
reaching out to Adam
atop the humble vault
of the human soul
now, at last, laid bare
of everything
but the soul's resolve
to claim life   in the next   breath

INTO THE SILENCE

On a perfect night
such as this
not so very long ago
beseeching the desert-clear stars
arrayed in the same constellations
I see above me tonight
I stretched up my arms
filled my legs with earth
and cried out
with a voice full of avalanches and earthquakes
the ferocity of lions, the soul-harrowing of wolves
the most savage sound I have ever heard
coming from depths so laden
with anguish upon anguish upon anguish
that all of life's attendant hurts
seemed to rise up in me. My family
and the families before my family
the ranks of my ancient ancestors
all roused to a singular chorus
a wail of heart-rending sorrow
so immense
only the vast and empty darkness
of the night sky could contain it.

In the resonant layers of that cry
I felt the strains of countless anonymous lives
calling out through me
the meager disowned parts
pleading to be heard, seeking
finally to be set free.

Then, inevitably, with nothing left to surrender
I commended my soul to the crushing
    silence
    of the starry night
    and when my voice died
    in that silence
        so did
            I

PASSING

On my rounds today
I come upon a broken stile
in my pasture fence. It has red threads
caught in its splintered claw—
a toll on the country walker
who'd wedged through, rather than climb
over, the old creosote post and rail.

This red remnant, otherwise so out of place
marks precisely where my red eyes
must search
for hints of the way he went.
I tell myself that if the trodden grass
had sifted his secrets
amongst its blades
I would have found them.
Nowhere is there a trace of blood—
only the innocent stile, sprung
by an uneasy passage.

My mind drifts, and I remember
that once-upon-a-time
my father lay out there on a cot
reading until sunset, so contented
he had to be called in
like a boy to supper.

A gentle hand of air touches my face
just as a kingbird lights on a nearby post
to watch for grasshoppers

as the wind ruffles
the newly mown field.

In the distant hills, I think I see
a trail winding up to the ridges.
Yet, it is but mid-day, and the sun urges
me onward. Mending this fence
and raking this hay
will fill the rest of my day.

THE MIND TURNS BACK

It's a story that could be true.
The body expires from whatever cause
and suddenly loses nearly an ounce—
the average weight of a human soul.
The chord breaks, and you are finally
free to fly, like an uncaged bird.
Light streams in, bearing welcome faces.
You must, of course, go with them.
Perhaps, there are life-reviews
with ascended Masters
or biding time as a hungry ghost
lurking in spectral households.

Time runs a thousand times slower
than in suburbs, or even dull poetry
and when you think of something
it magically appears, just like *that*.
You could teleport to Belize, simply
by setting foot in your mind's image.
Dreams prepare you for this afterlife.
Familiar, yet estranged, you are groomed
to become more subtle, more purely
the being of light you naturally are.

Crossing the bardo into the Mystery
you will be tempted as never before
to cling to Earth's heartbeat, desperately
as if to reclaim your own mortal heart.
This precious mother-child synchrony
endures fiercely, a bond too eternally
familiar to relinquish completely, despite

the angels, saints and celestial choirs
beseeching you with rapturous melodies
so pure, a single note contains more bliss
than you've ever known—alluring music
bereft of flesh and shed of all else but Spirit.

Your already famished heart
rummages through its bone yard
craving the blood that always filled it.
The soul hesitates, though its effulgence
beckons, because the mind would rather
turn back than let itself go blank
and the heart, like a bodhisattva
goes wherever it's most needed.

DOVE COTTAGE

Grasmere, England

Flagstone floors, dark wood paneling
the smallness of the space itself . . .
hardly what I expected
given the enormity of Wordsworth
and my expectations.
How could this cramped cottage
hold him . . . and all of them?
The lakes, hills, hedgerows and copses
that haunt the poet's words?
The faraway meadows of Tintern
sloping down to the river Wye?

Touch the whitewashed walls
on the second floor, your face turned
towards the window's meager light
then let your restless muse burst past
these confinements.
The brave have long flown the dovecote
to risk the open spaces, where falcons
burst birds into silent explosions.

Stand anywhere, soften your eyes
and you can feel the goddess
indwelling this countryside
her ardor already ravaging your skin.
At once, your heart must stretch
wide to embrace this world.

Feel her hand lightly on your back
prodding you out into the countryside
where you must make your way on foot
as if the only way to know, to truly know
these living earthly realms
is to be out walking.
You need no other spur than
the *élan vital* of any able creature.

Feel the company of souls gathered
eager for the long walk to Rydal
along road and brook, past gates
and stiles and pastures of mewling sheep.
Mind your footfall crushing elfin webs
between the hoarfrost leaves, glistening
in morning's golden light, where the last
of the fall warblers can be heard
but not seen, in the bending alder trees
along the trail to White Moss.
Stand in stillness often and long
listening for the song that will rise up
inside you
the one you alone can hear.

SACRED HEARTS

Whenever I visit Stella Maris Church
where in childhood I served as altar boy
it's like draping myself with a cloak
made of my heart's memories.
On any weekday afternoon
I'll likely be the only visitor.
Though not much a church-goer
I am drawn to *this* church
like a pilgrim to a shrine.
Amazed at myself, I linger over blessing
with holy water, I genuflect slowly
then softly walk over to say hello
to my old friend Joseph, standing off
on the right side of the chapel.

On the left side, my old friend, the Risen Jesus
casts his gaze introspectively
wistfully, towards the ground.
Tilting his sublime face, he points
to his Sacred Heart with a hand
that still gapes open with a dark nail slit.
From the top of his exposed Heart
a rosette of fire flares upward
fueling an alchemy of liberation
forever flaming forth into phoenix.

Note the golden glow, the fierce
spears of lightning, radiating
from his Heart, as his ecstatic soul
reposes in the afterglow
of the human body's fulfillment.

It feels necessary that he
remain there
holding vigil
necessary
that he point the way of the Sacred Heart
with that mysterious wisp
of melancholy.

At the main altar Mary holds up her baby
at the level of her heart
as though formally presenting him
to the world as her labor of love.
Even as a toddler, his mission streams
through his out-stretched, cherubic arms.
Note the mudra formed by his tiny
prescient hand, blessing untold souls
with long-awaited mercy.

Mary smiles mysteriously, reconciled
it seems, to the sorrows of this world.
Her Mona Lisa smile
seems redolent of visions
that cannot and need not be spoken.
Hail Mary, Mother of God, I repeat.
Of course, I've repeated that prayer
a thousand times, but these days
it's often down to just those few words
Hail Mary, Mother of God
. . . delightfully iconoclastic
in a Catholic-Buddhist sort of way.

To the many faithful candles
flickering before her, I have come
to light my own, not asking for anything
but in greeting, the way a son
greets his own mother, when, after years
of being man and father, his heart
forgives life all its messiness, and his face
often wears her subtle smile.

WHY I MUST FEEL HER DEEPLY NOW

The deepest experience of the Creator is Feminine
—Rainer Maria Rilke

Even my calmest mind
has shifted its intent
from lofty perch to everything I feel
happening in this world
with its stumbling traffic and dirty air
the species dying and the melting poles
ethnic cleansing and jihad
violence at the hands of men
homeless children and their mothers
and I could go on, but really
what I feel is not a list of grievances
but a massive desecration
unfolding right now in front of me.

How am I to be, and what am I to do?

My meditations now seek to lighten
the burdens of this Earth
its slums and tenements
its bombed out villages
its jungles littered with landmines
its poisoned rivers and despoiled seas.

My soul refuses to ascend
my soul refuses to ascend
but lingers on the filthy trail
I have unconsciously abetted.

My soul learned of itself
from tender women
whose hearts have suffered to excess.

Do not ask why I must feel Her deeply now
because I have learned to look around
and feel the horror of her absence.

INTO THE UNKNOWN SEA

For David Whyte

I have heard Mermaids signing
on the shore of dreams.

Remember you are not alone
when your soul casts off her moorings.
Even after a lifetime spent preparing
you will be frightened and at first
plagued with doubt, as you cross
this last isthmus into the unknown sea.
The portmanteau of your many selves
with their many-errand lives
provisioned now for all your needs, except
the ones your mind craves most, the very ones
your wise soul rejects—the maps
to which you have always clung
the plans that always kept you safe
the cages that can no longer contain
who you need to become.

Remember you are not alone
whatever might arise, your vessel
has been crafted to explore Originality
so fierce its mission, even gods
in their celestial estates would rouse
to cheer you on had they the human heart
to hold our common feelings. Your courage

has been a covenant since the birth of time
guiding you to this verge of becoming
where the scales could tip either way
the pivot of everything you hold most dear.

Remember you are not alone
as the doors close behind you
sealing all hope of exit or reprieve.
Then, patiently waiting as the water deepens
you will feel your heart stretched
wider than ever before
to hold your soul's vast pregnancy.
Breathe deeply the first foreign scents
rising in the morning mist, as if
all this time the native genius
you long sought elsewhere
lay hidden in your body.

Remember you are not alone
as the waters rise one level to the next.
Your soul has forever yearned
for this one gift—
that your mind un-selve its enormity
awakening the full-blooded Earthling
made of living soil
hills, meadows, surging rivers and clouds
that rub their bodies into lightening.

IV

there is still
somewhere deep within you
a beast shouting that the earth
is exactly what it wanted—
—Mary Oliver

Photo by author
Mary Magdalene chapel on a mountain cliff
near Le Puy, France

STAY THE LONG NIGHT

Slack tide and the stalled
breath of marshy vapors
the reeking compost
of exposed mud flats
the clacking of oysters
the squawk of a rousted heron
the slap of a jumping mullet
and then, inevitably
in that stillness that resists stillness
a faint riffle
of ocean breeze
whisks together a mouthful of flavors
familiar as aromas
from my mother's kitchen
distilled into a jot of rapture
so intense
I need only stay the long night
to be reborn.

So I remain a tidal sacristan
a contented creature
perched on the water's edge
watching the stars spill
onto the shoreline
in constellations of fireflies
spreading currents of ecstasy
as the water gathers
the owl's ghostly voice
the nightjar's whistle
and the maddened chorus of cicadas.

A sudden gust
plays the pines like harp strings
and my bones hum along
remembering an ancient melody
arising from the earth's
not so distant core
and an invisible filament of fire
ignites in my heart
from the friction of flesh and spirit.

In my heart's hands
even the smallest spark
burns whatever in me is dry, leaving ashes
only tears can dissolve
and only the tides can reclaim.
In the heart's long vigil, my roots deepen
and I become
more simply earth, more simply fire.

THE EMPTY BEACH

I let my mind swim naked
because the choir of hollow reeds
must displace the traffic of thinking
I brought with me from the city.

Stinging sands gust over the beach
yet I welcome them, because
my heart knows to stand its ground
till drifts gather round my ankles.

The wind presses the ocean's
roaring wilderness into my body
harrowing the frail plotlines
of the stories that sustain me.

If I let the ocean remind my
blood of its source, quite easily
I close my eyes and rest my head
upon that ceaseless heartbeat.

On the empty beach with no sense
of self, I learn to take my place
among the hollow reeds and let
the wind move through me.

Photo by author
HH Dalai Lama's residence in India

A SUITE OF CREATURE SONGS

Today, my mind
shot through
an open window
to a nearby tree
      to a singing bird.

On the bird were
bright feathers.

In the feathers were
lice   as fine as dust.
On the lice were
mites   tinier than pinpoints.

In the eye of one mite
was the thousand-mile stare

of a god in the making.

This cricket-voice in my right ear
came from a music before my soul
was startled into being with light
before mind and void began
beckoning to each other.

Beyond all origins
is the source of this
cricket-voice singing
and this awareness in me

that hears it, when
no-cricket-voice
is the One singing.

Even the most sublime
transports of my mind
proclaim how thoroughly
I am Earthen—in each stretch
of imagination, some sway
of Earth's pulse, some ripple
through layers of her flesh
through soil, sea and air
exhorting all creatures
as cells of one body
to flow with Life unhindered
answering the call
to be her eye and ear
reaching outward to embrace
daughter moon and the fire
of sun and stars, reaching
at last inward
to join the chorus
of creature songs
whose only song
is the Love of this one Life.

MOTIONLESS WINGS

Sullivan's Island, South Carolina

Two freighters at anchor
in the mouth of the harbor
alongside the shipping lanes.
A quilt of gray overhead.
The drab silhouette of the city
in the misty distance.
I perch, hunched into a ball
on rocks near the ruins of an old fort.
Storm waves fling their frigid spray
in my direction, crashing on the jetty's
eroded boulders—
my own callow roughness
worn smooth, by grief
more than joy.

I wonder about the lives
of the people aboard those freighters
pitched and yawed by winter's grind.
Are there women on bunks
tucked into those hulls?
Are there men onboard
inured to everything
but the rhythm of the sea?
Or, do they crave and pace
and wobble in their dreams?

Even in the winter toss
the usual tour boats cruise

and sport-fishers set out.
A pod of dolphins, three abreast
followed by others three-abreast
keeps a brisk pace, arching in unison.
What is it like to be them?
Why do I yearn to know
with the same fire
as knowing myself?

In the buffeting headwind
the sheath of unknowing
unfurls its hidden wings
and I soar
with avian eyes
and bones of light.

SECRET ATTRACTION

Past the beached bateau and the trail of deep
    gouges, a man waded knee-deep
in the river, behind the veil of a cast net.

From a dock on the other side, fingering
    the pulse of crab lines, a woman
watched and wondered if she knew him.

His face was hidden by the oblique sun
    as he attended the refracted light
postulating shadows into the evening catch.

She raised her hand, as a question
    formed on her face, then, just as quickly
felt her heart wilt and wondered why.

One day, after months of declining invitations
    each accustomed to solitude, and
wary of their hosts' well-meaning motives

the man uncharacteristically agreed
    to dinner, and this once the woman
allowed herself to be persuaded.

That night, the man's indelible river mud
    was already flecked with the woman's
phosphorescence, and from its tilting cup

the conspiring moon kept pouring
    its armor-piercing glitter
onto their unsuspecting bodies

until each felt a familiar presence
    turned, and saw each other
for the first time.

HIEROS GAMOS UNDER THE MOON

Springtime's full moon
spilt her spectral sheen
of luminous, opalescent milk
all over my body, so intensely, I quivered
as though upon me lay the drizzled
essence of woman.

My transfigured skin shone silver-scaled
with shiver-waves, lapping the shores
of the night's indigo sea.
So . . . I undressed for her, slowly
as my bare skin took on
her supernal luster.

My naked body
like a stranger, stirred
with a wild-amorous urge
to seek out and merge
with a dream-lover, hidden
somewhere in the long, dark shadows.

Already driven wild by the moon's caresses
my body and my mind so craved
to ravage a woman's body
I rolled in the grasses
plunged into the nearby pond
and jutted my sex without a thought
till I saw its shadow
in the moonlight.

The conspiring flowers
exuded their aphrodisia
into the iridescent darkness
as the world fell under the moon's spell
and all beings, seen and unseen
dared to be naked and love-crazed
as if Earth herself were a bawdy mistress
and all of Life her raucous, writhing body.

Photo by author
Mary Magdalene, St Maximin, France

THE ART OF EATING GRAPES
On the TGV to Avignon

An old woman sitting alone
aslant before the window
gazes beyond the blur
eating grapes in pure abandonment.
Her head lolls back and
I notice her eyelids flutter
as if some carnal genius
were ravishing her body.
The still-folded, reticent napkin
blots her minutely quivering lips.

Slowly, she spits
seeds onto a teaspoon
and I feel my heart opening
as if I am witnessing
the machinations of a truth
somehow vital to all of life
as if, in the end, her
un-self-conscious way
would always triumph.

Then, at the climax
the spoon's sharp clink
against the porcelain saucer
pierces me
like a cosmic high note

and in a flash
the glistening seeds, still warm
from her mouth, leap through
the third eye of my humble muse
and my heart, aroused, holds her
in its arms for dear life.

LAUNCHED INTO THE INFINITE YEARS

For Sensei Bonnie Myotai Treace

Was it amid the shadows of the moon
one night long ago that you first felt
and then somehow knew
you were caught-up in the ripples
of the body attuning itself
to its own in-between-ness?

It does not matter how

the inevitable arrives out of nowhere
or how like a lurking stranger
this presence at first might disturb you.
Clearly, unmistakably, it has traversed
vast chasms of the unrememberable
to haunt you with something
not even a poem can hold on to.

And, of course, all of this is
quite different from the years
that measure you—

though, they do arrive as well
and with them a blessed, irascible knack
for savoring the sweet spots
like the jolt of the first few molecules
of truly wicked dark chocolate
ravaging your hapless taste buds—
how like a holy terror the taste
spreads through your body
until, gasping, you realize

you've been gunned down
and are now helplessly writhing
in a pool of your own rapture.

TEA WITH NERUDA

The teakettle is barely warm. *Mi bonita esposa*
    has already consumed the silent hours.
And now, though not yet dawn, the kitchen is hardly quiet.
    The ceiling fan, a few cars, the refrigerator
my mind, all have their motors toiling away.
    Pablo, I made a bookmark for you last night
from a postcard, by cutting along the voluptuous edges
    of a dark woman, including (*pero claro*)
    the full extent of her endearing, pendulous shadow.
    You will appreciate that her swollen-plum lips
have begun to dye your words
    with their ripe juices
and her drooping eyes
lure your tropes away from their tasks
to look
wherever she is looking.
I think you will weep
    as we are interrupted
    by the kettle's wounded harmonica
    at the precise moment
the indispensable fire truck
    rounds the corner, screaming
    that for us there can never be any illusions
of isolation.
    No doubt, your heart will be pierced, as mine is
    by the flawlessly orchestrated, peerless beauty
of the suddenly pregnant
    bulge
    of silence
into which my nineteen year-old son now stumbles
(at the very crowning of the golden dawn no less!)

pleading for a ride to his biology class
because his bicycle was struck by a car yesterday
    now funny to him, because the drowsy driver
    is a girl
he'd like to date. And, dear friend, if you can bear it—
    the mystery-woman's silhouette
    is really the artist's self-portrait
disguised as a loitering passerby
    reflected in her gallery's window.

PEACE OF HEART

When you find peace within yourself, you become the kind of person who can live at peace with others.
—Peace Pilgrim

When I put my opinions aside
for a long-enough while, and look
unflinching with curiosity and care
I see that everything that *can* exist
struggles *to* exist, to come into being
in whatever form for however long
in this dance of possibility.

There are lessons
heaped upon lessons, no matter
how far I have come.
I want to learn from everything
and count all life as precious
without judging it awry
or somehow expendable.

Some Witness in me
urges my hand
to tuck the exposed worm
back into its bed of soil
as though it were
a precious child.

Perhaps I am still haunted
by death and loss
or just ignorant of my motive.

Yet, I know my peace of heart
is where this Witness resides.

I hope you do not mind
if I take it with me
wherever I go.

PROPOSAL

See this hand of mine
weathered and thinner
than when we first met
more wracked with age
no doubt less ambitious
than when I was full of appetites
though in fairness, a hand . . .
well, let me presume to say, a hand less hasty
more thoughtful
and kindly disposed—
a pardonably seasoned hand
reddened by autumn days
and no less by autumn years
yet a thoroughly serviceable hand
broad and strong, grown tender
and perhaps more attentive.
My hand does flow with a man's rough blood
but also with the blood of rivers, earth and tears
with muscles of conscience
and bones of alloys
light enough for flight
yet rooted here in love.
See this hand of mine?
Here, as it is, I offer it to you.

Photo by author
Namgyal Monastery, Dharamsala, India

Women have a special capacity to lead us to a more peaceful world with compassion, affection and kindness. And there is no more important time for that than this moment.
——HH Dalai Lama

IN A CIRCLE OF WOMEN

For Jean Shinoda Bolen

After each has said the who and why, and
        bared the bones that lead to sisterhood
a tender mood enfolds them in its loving quilt
        as each turns to face the juicy crone
the elder-woman at the circle's core, the midwife
        who will guide them through their labors
not merely for themselves, but for the Earth.
        They've come to drink this woman in
to catch her manna, to feed the growing body
        whose girth is now a circle of women.
Wake up, wake up, a gentle voice insists, *you must*
        open like a flower, because *she*
calls forth a hidden Oneness, a gathering, a presence
        stirring beneath your closed petals
whose nectar, even now, you begin to taste

        Then suddenly, it is your turn to speak.
You must make your declaration. Except, this time
        you've not rehearsed a thing to say
and you must awaken from your trance.
        No more room for hiding
nor berth for the sleeper who'd not be roused.

        All-at-once you need no further
urging, your heart surging for the final push
        as you take that fated lung-full
that will coax from deep inside
        the new life you have yearned for
        from which

        there is no turning back.

ACKNOWLEDGEMENTS

At the top of my list, my love and deep appreciation for my wife, Carolyn Rivers, for her tireless encouragement and inspiration.

I very likely would not have pursued this particular poetry project were it not for the support and loving encouragement of Sue Monk Kidd, Terry Helwig and Susan Hull Walker.

My deep gratitude for fellow poets David Whyte, Mark Nepo and Kurt Lamkin, friends, mentors and champions of Art that flows from Heart. My deep gratitude to Mark Nepo, Susan Hull Walker and Harriet McDougal for their editorial genius.

Artist and illustrator Cristina Young for all of the skill and patience she brought to the book formatting process.

The Poetry Society of South Carolina for "Woman," which won the Society's Best Lyric Poem prize in 2005

Omar Sobhani and Thomson-Reuters for the photograph of the veiled Afghan woman in Kabul

Thomas Locke Hobbs for the photograph of La Difunta Correa shrine site in Patagonia

Carrie Allen McCray Nickens, now deceased, for her own photograph